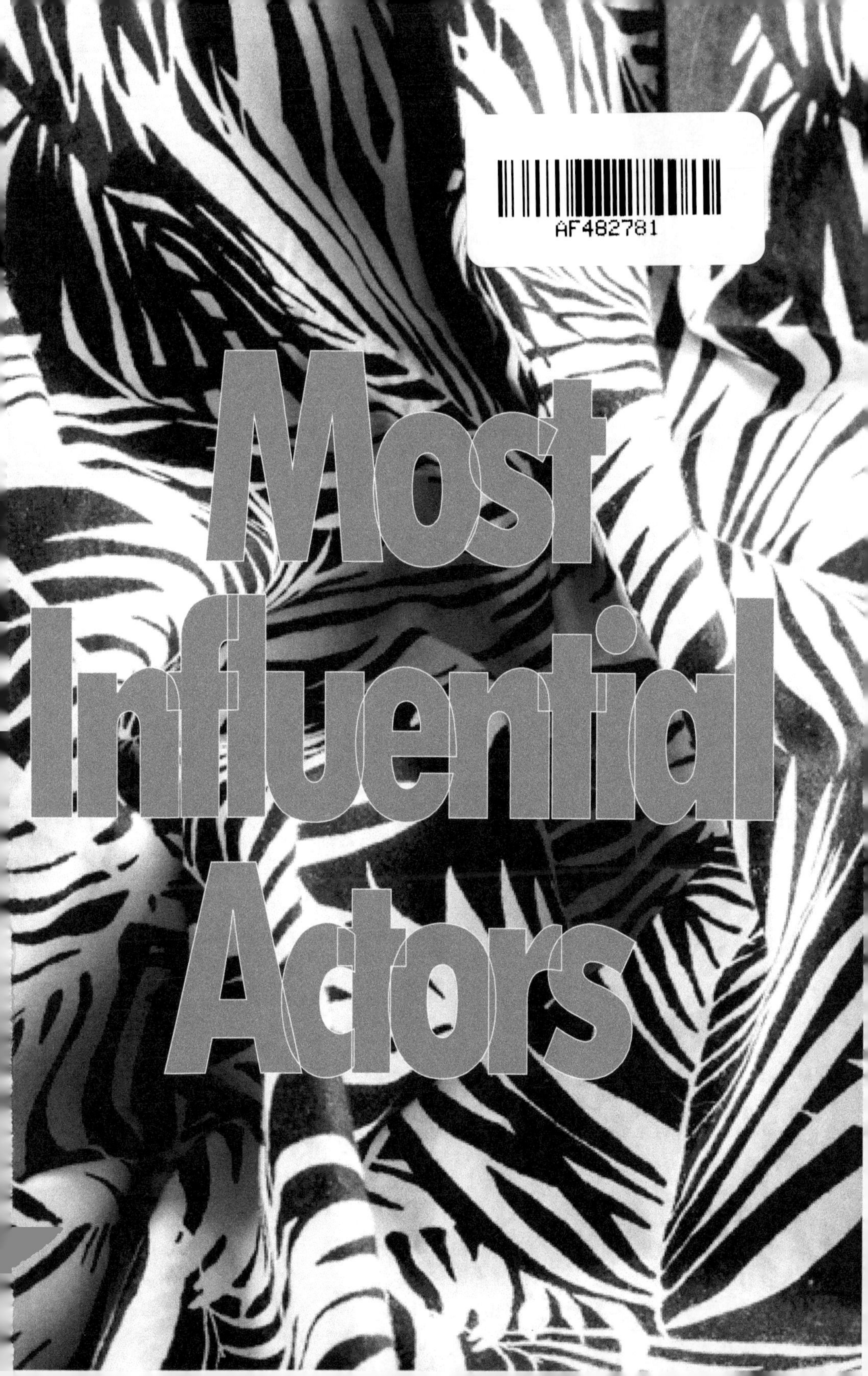

AF482781
Most
Influential
Actors

# Most Influential Actors

# Table Of Contents

# Foreword

*Somebody once said that you can't get inspired in a vacuum. You require outside influences to help activate the process. The Greeks had their Muses, spirits and goddesses, who inspired the creation of the arts. Claude Monet had his haystacks. Every person, great and small requires inspiration and every person is inspired by different matters.*

*Movies and the actors in them may be just as inspirational as the real world. Often people get ideas for a fresh path or creative idea by watching movies or the actors that appear in them. Content may vary widely and it truly depends upon the interests of the person. You may be inspired by a work of utter fiction or you may like historic or biographic material. Whatever your pastime, there's a movie or actor out there that may supply inspiration.*

*Most Inspiring Actors*

*Discover How To Develop Fame And Fortune By Learning From The Best!*

# Chapter 1:

*Sarah Jessica Parker*

# Synopsis

*The Sex and the City celebrity was the youngest of 4 youngsters born into a struggling family in an Ohio coal-mining township. Her parents split up when she was two; before long, her mother remarried and had 4 more youngsters. With a lot of mouths to feed, her homemaker mother and trucker stepfather fought to get by. Parker's way to stardom started early, however, when she landed her beginning Broadway role at eleven, and traveled to Hollywood in '81 to appear on the television program Square Pegs. The actress is reportedly worth more than $one hundred thirty million now.*

# **Starting Early**

Parker started working at age eight, acting the lead in an after-school special shot in her hometown of Cincinnati. 3 years later, in '76, she got her first Broadway play, The Innocents. At thirteen, arrived the head role in Annie. Other work came after, achieving a career high with HBO's Sex and the City. She's acted in twenty-three movies, including The Family Stone, for which she was named for a Golden Globe.

"Nothing in life comes easy," she has said. "You have to earn everything." So you have to recognize the difference between what you wish and what you require. "I always knew I needed to work."

"Work was never about wanting fame or money," she has also stated. She loves getting the job, attending rehearsals, lounging with a bunch of actors. "I needed that the way you need water", she has said. She needed to act.

She is the youngest of 4 children born into a struggling family in Nelsonville, Ohio, a coal-mining township. Her mother quit a teaching job to raise her 5 sons and 3 daughters.

Parker wasn't brought up with money and privilege. Her biologic dad was a poet. Her mom was busy with 8 youngsters, and her dad was on the road. Parker has said a large part of not being affluent as a child isn't that you haven't the stuff you wish. It isn't living without heat or the telephone. It's resting in bed in the dark, thinking about your parents' worries.

Parker has said that she's thankful for all that now. It acquainted her with a good work ethic and understanding for the bulk of individuals, who aren't affluent. She feels in touch with their lives because of the way she was raised.

Once she was eleven, the household moved to the Greater New York region. Sarah got a role in The Innocents. The experience altered her life. The star of the show took her under her wing. Before every performance, she'd go up to the stars dressing room and watch her sit, strikingly lovely in her bathrobe, spritzing Evian water on her skin. Parker would listen to her perfect diction and think, that is all I want—merely to be like her!

While she might not have looked for wealth or celebrity, Parker, has earned both.

In '91 Parker's career arrived at a major landmark with the charmingly quirky romantic comedy L.A. Story. For the 1st time, she acted as a target of desire, and that got roles in films like Honeymoon in Vegas and made her a celebrity.

Nowadays, Parker participates in children's charities, bringing in funds for New York public schools and functioning as an ambassador for UNICEF. She does this because of her own experiences as a youngster. Parker has said she's learned that your childhood doesn't have to prescribe the rest of your life if you're afforded skills, opportunity and self-sufficiency..

# Chapter 2:

*Oprah Winfrey*

# Synopsis

*Born in Mississippi to young, unmarried parents, Oprah Winfrey was brought up by her grandma till she was six years old, when her guardian got ill. Winfrey then relocated to Milwaukee to live with her mom and half-sister in a boarding house. Oprah's mom, who worked as a maid, banked on welfare now and then to support the family. Winfrey marched on to become a hardworking businesswoman, metamorphosing herself from news anchor to talk-show host to leader of her own multiplatform media conglomerate..*

# Faith

A calculating and responsible businesswoman, Oprah has turned her initial success in TV into many other ventures, including the conception of her own production company. In spite of her now fabled Midas touch – celebrity, power, and riches virtually bound from all of her projects – Oprah has another view of her position; for her, success is "getting to the point where you're absolutely comfortable with yourself ... to have the sort of internal strength and inner courage it takes to say, 'No, I won't let you treat me this way' is what success is all about."

Her travel to this self-realization hasn't been simple.

Winfrey's mom and dad, unmarried, were teenagers when she was born in Mississippi. She was given the name Orpah after an adult female from the Book of Ruth but a spelling error on the birth certificate altered it to Oprah. She passed her childhood growing up in miserable poverty on her profoundly religious grandma's farm. When she was a little older, Winfrey moved in with her mom in Milwaukee, WI.

This turned out to be a difficult time as Winfrey says she was repeatedly sexually molested by male relatives. Winfrey got to be a bit of a wild youngster during her early teens, trying out sex and drugs till the age of fourteen when she birthed a premature infant. It died not long after, and upon recuperating, Winfrey decided to live with her dad in Nashville. It was under his strict guidance that Winfrey discovered discipline, constancy, and the inspiration to excel in school and alter her life.

Oprah has said that in her total life experience, her ability to believe in herself, and even in her blackest moments of sexual assault and being physically ill-treated etc., she knew there was a different way. She knew there was a formula to get out. She knew there was a different sort of life because she had read about it. She knew there were other places, and there was a different way of existence. It preserved her life, so that's why she now focuses her attention on attempting to do the same thing for others.

Oprah's rise to celebrity started when she took over a local Chicago talk show, which shortly became The Oprah Winfrey Show. In '85 she completed her dream of becoming an actress, making critical acclaim and getting an Academy Award nomination for her support role as Sophia in the film The Color Purple. A year afterward her show went to the number one talk show.

The fame of the show stems from Oprah's emotion, vulnerability, and compassionateness as a host and interviewer. She was the first to build an extra connection with her audience by sharing her personal life, ranking from anecdotes about her life partner Stedman Graham, to her emotional revealing of her own childhood sexual assault.

Fantastic material success has let Oprah pursue other things that very matter ... being able to create a difference ... in others lives. She also supports educational initiatives and those who help other people in their communities.

# Chapter 3:

*Jim Carrey*

# Synopsis

*Born and brought up in Canada, Jim Carrey was a senior high dropout whose household fell on hard times when he was an adolescent. With his dad laid off, Carrey assisted in paying the bills by doing work as a janitor and a security guard. Yet, the family finally lost their home, and was forced to live in a van. After relocating to the U.S. and struggling on the comedy clubs in LA, Carrey broke it big on the TV program In Living Color. Forbes says he today realizes around $20 million per movie.*

# Determination

Arguably the top screen comic of the '90s, Canadian-born entertainer Jim Carrey has blended equivalent parts of his idol Jerry Lewis, his unearthly ancestor Harry Ritz, and the loose-limbed Ray Bolger into a joyfully uninhibited screen persona that's uniquely his own.

Carrey's life was not always a barrelful of laughs; he was born on Jan 17, 1962, into a peripatetic home that on a regular basis ran the gamut from middle-class comfortableness to miserable poverty. Not amazingly, Carrey became a classic overachiever, standing out in academics while keeping his schoolmates in stitches with his tempestuous improvisations and elastic facial gestures.

His comedy club unveiling at age sixteen was a grim failure, but Carrey had already decided not to be beaten down by life's letdowns (as his dad, a disappointed musician, had been). By age twenty-two, he was making a quality living as a standup comedian, and was starring on the short-lived sitcom The Duck Factory -- a serial which oddly did little to capitalize on its star's weird physical dexterity.

Throughout the eighties, Carrey appeared in support roles in such movies as Peggy Sue Got Married ('86) and Earth Girls are Easy ('90). Full TV stardom came Carrey's way in '90 as the main "white guy" on Keenan Ivory Wayans' Fox television comedy In Living Color.

The most popular of the comics many portrayals on the program was the monstrously disfigured Fire Marshal Bill, whose doubtful safety tips imposed the wrath of real world fire prevention groups -- and likewise earned Carrey the ultimate award of being copied by other comedians.

He wrote himself a check for 10 million dollars for acting services delivered and dated it Thanksgiving Day '95. He put it in his wallet and it fell apart. Then, just prior to Thanksgiving '95, he discovered he was going to make 10 million bucks for Dumb & Dumber. He put that check in the coffin with his father as it was their dream together.

Carey has said he hasn't been as wild with his money as someone like him might have been. He's been very safe, really conservative with investments. He doesn't blow money. He doesn't have a ton of houses. He recognizes things may go away because he's already had that experience. He was and remains determined..

# Chapter 4:

*Demi Moore*

# Synopsis

- 18 -

*Demi, Demetria Guynes, who was born in Roswell, New Mexico, was raised in a trailer park by her alcohol-dependent mother and stepfather. The 2 had a fierce relationship and oftentimes moved the household around the country. Moore finally threw in the towel where school was concerned at sixteen to quest after modeling. She relocated to Europe for an abbreviated period and got married to rocker Freddie Moore at eighteen. Her discovery came a year later, when she got a spot on General Hospital. There are reports that she's worth an approximated $75 million nowadays.*

# Level Head

Moore led a pained childhood. To call it troubled would be something of an understatement: her biological father left her mother after just 2 months of wedlock. Along with her mother, half-brother and stepfather, she relocated many times before her adolescence, thanks to her stepfather's occupation as a newspaper advertisement salesman.

The troubles that went along with such a traveling lifestyle were heightened by the dysfunctional, occasionally abusive relationship between Moore's mom and stepfather.

Her home life was crazy, destabilized by constant battles between her alcohol-dependent parents. It wasn't till she was in her teens that Moore found out who her real dad was. Her step father committed suicide when she was fifteen, around the time that she distinguished that he wasn't her biological father. She threw in the towel at school a year later and did a little modeling in Europe.

Once she was eighteen, she married rocker Freddy Moore; the marriage lasted 4 years, during which time the actress got her first role playing Jackie Templeton on the television daytime drama General Hospital.

Moore likewise suffered grievous medical problems as a youngster. She was cross-eyed and for a time and wore an eye patch, till a surgery corrected the issue. She likewise almost died from a renal disorder.

But these feelings of childhood insufficiency produced a mighty ambition in her, which discovered a focus when a friend, the actress Nastassja Kinski, hinted she ought to attempt acting.

It makes an incredible feeling of drive towards overcoming, establishing you're of value, that you've a purpose and a sense of worth, Demi has said. "The trouble comes when you cannot let go of the youngster in you that nevertheless needs that approval. She thinks the hard times she had in her childhood also gave her the potency to cope with a lot of other things in her life. She has said that those are the things that give us the colors that make us who we are.

She has said that that the focus on her body got obsessional and unhealthy. She thinks it stemmed from a longing for approval induced by her traumatic childhood. Dysfunction or trouble in childhood truly produces such a tremendous lack of self-respect and self-confidence, she has said.

You have to discover a sense of value that comes from inside, not, as it was occasionally for me, Moore has said, from self-importance, from outside things like success in a career. But that's difficult when you grow up without a feeling of self-worth.

# Chapter 5:

*Tom Cruise*

# Synopsis

*Another youngster of a struggling single mother, Cruise's household moved frequently so his mom, a special education instructor, could get work. She reportedly bore up to 4 jobs at a time to support her youngsters. Ultimately taking root in New Jersey, Cruise discovered a safe harbor in the theater department of his high school, which he threw in the towel during his senior year to go after acting. At the time of his split up from Nicole Kidman in 2003, it was approximated he was responsible for $250 million of their $350 million wealth.*

# Create Who You Are

The name has become synonymous with all-American testosterone-driven amusement. Tom Cruise spent the eighties as one of Hollywood's brightest-shining wonder boys.

With black hair, blue eyes, and unembarrassed forwardness, Cruise rode richly on such hits as Top Gun and Rain Man. While his popularity dipped slightly in the early 'nineties, he was able to get over it with a chain of hits that reinstated him as both an action hero and, in the case of Jerry Maguire and Magnolia, a gifted actor.

Cruise, born Thomas Cruise Mapother IV, was raised in near poverty in a Catholic family reigned by an abusive father he named as "a merchant of chaos." His dad was an electrical engineer who could never hold down an occupation and kept the household on the move in an uneasy search for work. His mom, Mary Lee Mapother South, fought to support the household.

Cruse has said he was a bully and a coward, of the father who beat him. He was the sort of individual where, if something fails, they kick you. It was a good lesson in my life—how he'd lull you in, makes you feel safe then, bam! For me, it was like, 'There's something amiss with this man. Do not trust him. Be careful close to him. There's that tension.

As a boy, Cruise has stated, he was not able to read. Being in alterative classes departed from "normal" kids gave him vivid frustration. He felt left out. Little for his age, he was lonesome and eager to be liked. Rather, he was pushed around regularly in the fifteen different schools he went to in twelve years.

Individuals may produce their own lives, he has said. He saw how his mom produced hers and so made it conceivable for them to pull through. His mom was the one who ascended to the occasion. She bore 3 jobs. She would say, 'We're going to get through this.'

Cruise has said he determined that he's going to produce, for himself, who he is, not what others say he ought to be. I'm entitled to that.

Tom Cruise's success is tremendous. The global gross of his more than twenty-four movies is now over $5.5 billion.

# Chapter 6:

*Tom Hanks*

# Synopsis

*Hanks is placed as the highest all time ticket office star with over $3.639 billion total ticket office gross, an average of $107 million per movie. He's been involved with 17 films that grossed over $100 million at the global ticket office. The highest grossing film he's starred in is 2010's Toy Story. He grew up in what he calls a "fractured" household. His parents were pioneers in the evolution of marriage dissolution law in their state, and Tom traveled a lot, living with a succession of step-families.*

# Pick What's Right For You

Hanks is placed as the highest all time ticket office star with over $3.639 billion total ticket office gross, an average of $107 million per movie. He's been involved with 17 films that grossed over $100 million at the global ticket office. The highest grossing film he's starred in is 2010's Toy Story. He grew up in what he calls a "fractured" household. His parents were pioneers in the evolution of marriage dissolution law in their state, and Tom traveled a great deal, living with a succession of step-families.

Tom Hanks is among those American actors who have wangled a way to carve a niche for themselves in the movie industry. He's mainly recognized for his intense roles, like those in 'Philadelphia', 'Forrest Gump', 'Saving Private Ryan' and 'Cast Away'. Aside from acting, he's also involved in directing, voice-overs, writing and film production. He is among the only 3 actors who have accomplished the feat of making 7 consecutive US$100 million blockbusters, till now. In 2006, he was placed as #1 in the 1,500 -strong list of 'Most Trusted Celebrities' accumulated by 'Forbes' magazine.

Hanks has said about choosing parts that he thinks there's an excessive amount of pressure as the risks are so immense. And if you do not have an instinctual association with the part, if you don't have some kind of constituent piece of yourself that's also there on the page and bounds forth, then you are going to be making a error. He also thinks it's very simple to fall into the ...I should do this sort of a part, I should do that sort of a part, and I ought to be playing much more to my fortes.

There is a Tom Hanks guideline when he looks at a script to decide if it's for him or not:

He says you have to have a base. He kind of still thinks of it like he did when reading books and writing compositions in high school. What is the base of this? What is it stating about the human condition, first of all, the American circumstance, 2nd, and your circumstance, 3rd? He always looks for that. Then afterwards, it's the additional material is like, who else is he going to have a chance to work for? What is it that he gets to do that he's done well earlier? What is it he gets to do in a particular script that he's never been able to do earlier? Then you have a good chance of picking a winning project...

# Wrapping Up

We're only too familiar with a lot of rags to riches stories hither and thither. But what do all these accounts bear in common? The tale of despair, poverty, promise, survival and overcoming the odds.... particularly when it's a movie star that we can go watch on the big screen.

What does it all mean? These rags to riches accounts and stories that let us know how stars got there all inspire us. If they may accomplish it, so may we--for these stories are real and someplace between the lines of poverty and wanting to be a celebrity, there's forever an inkling of hope, of not surrendering in spite of the rough times. All these stars have their own story and they each inspire us in different ways... but they do inspire us.

Take what inspires you from these stars to get where you would like to be.

Produce word of mouth. Get an authority to lecture or teach a class like a personal trainer to the stars to show your buyers how to get abs like Arnold. Then call for the media, they're always seeking a good story.